SMART ABOUT Art

Vincent van Gogh

Sunflowers and Swirly Stars

The Sower
by Millet

by Joan Holub

Grosset & Dunlap   New York

For Lorie Ann Grover,
who's always willing to lend an ear—J.H.

Cover image: Vincent van Gogh, *The Starry Night*, 1889. Oil on canvas, 29 x 36¼". The Museum of Modern Art, New York. Acquired through the Lillie P. Bliss Bequest. Photograph © 2001 The Museum of Modern Art, New York.

Library of Congress Cataloging-in-Publication Data

Holub, Joan.
    Vincent van Gogh : sunflowers and swirly stars / by Joan Holub.
        p. cm. — (Smart about art)
      1. Gogh, Vincent van, 1853-1890—Juvenile literature. 2. Painters—Netherlands—Biography—Juvenile literature. [1. Gogh, Vincent van, 1853-1890. 2. Artists.]
    I. Title. II. Series.
      ND653.G7 H577 2001
      759.9492—dc21
      [B]   2001023102

ISBN 0-448-42521-1   O P Q R S T U V W X Y Z

From the desk of
Ms. Brandt

Dear Class,

Our unit on famous artists is almost over. I hope that you enjoyed it as much as I did.

I am excited to read your reports. Here are some questions that you may want to think about:

- Why did you pick your artist?

- If you could ask your artist 3 questions, what would they be?

- Did you learn anything that really surprised you?

Good luck and have fun!

Ms. Brandt

He made notes and drew pictures of people

So I wrote and drew pictures on the sides of my report!

Stories of the *not* rich and *not* famous

Did you think Vincent van Gogh got rich from being an artist? I did.

I heard on TV that one of his paintings sold for over $82 million. It is called *The Portrait of Dr. Gachet*.

Painting would be a cool way to earn lots of money. I thought van Gogh was lucky to have earned that much for just *one* picture. That is why I picked him for my artist.

This is Dr. Gachet.   He was Vincent's friend.

But then I found out the truth.
Van Gogh was poor his whole life! He
did not become famous until after he died.

When Vincent was a boy

Vincent

His brothers and sisters

Theo

Vincent van Gogh was born on March 30, 1853. He lived in a little town in Holland named Groot-Zundert.

His father was a preacher, and his mother was a housewife. There were six kids in his family. He was the oldest. I know what that's like. I have a little brother and a little sister. I am the oldest, too.

Self-portait, by Vincent van Gogh. 1889. Photo credit: Scala/Art Resource, NY.

Vincent painted this self-portrait. You can see his red hair, but not his freckles.

Vincent was 13 in this picture.

Vincent van Gogh at age 13. Photo credit: Amsterdam, van Gogh Museum (Vincent van Gogh Foundation)

Vincent's favorite brother was named Theo. Theo always tried to help him out of trouble. And Vincent got in plenty of that.

School was no fun for Vincent. He got bad grades and had a hard time making friends. He quit school when he was only sixteen.

I drew this picture of me by looking in the mirror. That is how Vincent painted his self-portrait, too.

My brother painted this self-portrait. → He is only four.

 Vincent gets lucky

This is the art gallery where Vincent worked.

Luckily, Vincent's uncle gave him a job at an art gallery in Holland. This was his first big break.

At home, Vincent didn't get to go to art museums. There weren't any art books around either. But at his new job, Vincent saw art all day long. So he really liked it. He was so good at his job that his boss gave him a promotion. He sent him to work in an art gallery in London, England. Things were looking up.

Dear Theo, I miss you. V.

Dear Theo, I had eggs for breakfast. V.

Dear Theo, I had fish for lunch. V.

Dear Theo, I had stew for supper. V.

Dear Theo, Today I sold 100 pictures! V.

Dear Theo, Do you like this drawing? V.

When Vincent moved away, I think he really missed Theo. Vincent wrote lots of letters to his brother. He drew pictures all around the edges of the paper. They were pictures of buildings and interesting things he saw. In those days, most people didn't have cameras. It's a good thing Vincent could draw.

Dear Theo, I saw a cool building. V.

Letter from Vincent to his brother Theo, Paris, 1875.
Photo credit: Amsterdam, van Gogh Museum (Vincent van Gogh Foundation)

Dear Theo, I saw a good painting today. V.

GOUPIL & C.ᴵᴱ
Editeurs Imprimeurs
ESTAMPES FRANÇAISES & ÉTRANGÈRES
Tableaux Modernes
RUE CHAPTAL, 9, PARIS.
Succursales à la Haye, Londres, Berlin, New-York.

Paris, le 24 Juli 1875

Waarde Theo,
Een paar dagen geleden kregen wij een Sch'
van de Nittis, een gezicht in London op een

Dear Theo, I saw another one. V.

Dear Theo, I am very busy at my job. V.

Dear Theo, Wow! I saw another one! V.

Vincent wrote this letter to Theo in Dutch, not English. At the top, he drew a picture.

Dear Theo, Hi! Longer letter later. V.

Dear Theo, I wish I had a camera. V.

Dear Theo, ① I haven't written in 2 whole days, (continued)

so I have ② a lot to tell you. I saw a cool dog, (continued)

an interesting ③ building, a nice tree, a cat, (continued)

and a ④ river. Love, V.

Dear Theo, I still miss you. V.

Vincent ~~mese~~ ~~mos~~ messes up

Soon Vincent was in trouble again. He fell in love with a woman who didn't love him back. He felt sad all the time. Sometimes he forgot to go to work. Guess what? He lost his job.

Now Vincent needed a new job. He tried being a teacher. That didn't work out. He tried selling books in a bookstore. That didn't work either. Then he tried to be a preacher. Nope.

Vincent felt like a failure when these jobs didn't work out.

Next, Vincent decided to be a painter.

He didn't start out as a great artist. Most artists begin painting when they're a lot younger than he was. Vincent had a lot of catching up to do.

He practiced by copying other artists at first. Two of his favorites were Rembrandt van Rijn and Jean François Millet. They painted with dark colors. So Vincent did, too.

The Sower
by Millet

Why was the
potato mad?

Because it
was in a stew.

The Potato Eaters, by Vincent van Gogh. 1885.
Photo credit: Amsterdam, van Gogh Museum (Vincent van Gogh Foundation)

Guess what the people in "The Potato Eaters" are eating?

Vincent wanted to paint pictures of things he cared about. There were lots of poor people in Vincent's neighborhood. He worried about them. He painted a picture of them and called it *The Potato Eaters*.

Vincent worked on the picture for months. He was proud of it. But the colors are dark, and the people look sad. I don't like it. Nobody else did either.

A hot potato

What do you call
a potato from Paris?

A French
Fry!

13

Time to Move

Vincent went to live in Paris, France, in 1886. He met lots of other artists there. Many of them, like Claude Monet, are famous today. But back then, they were just struggling artists like Vincent.

In Vincent's time, artists painted pictures to look real—almost like photographs. Some artists began experimenting. They put their feelings into their paintings. Their brushstrokes showed. These artists were nicknamed "Impressionists" because they painted their impressions of things they saw. People were shocked by their art.

Vincent made friends with artists named Paul Signac and Georges Seurat. They painted in a style called pointillism. Up close, their pictures look like a mess of dots. But from far away, they look like regular paintings.

Georges Seurat, French, 1859-1891, *A Sunday on La Grande Jatte* – 1884, oil on canvas, 1884-86, 207.6 x 308 cm, Helen Birch Bartlett Memorial Collection, 1926.224. Photograph © 2000, The Art Institute of Chicago, All Rights Reserved.

This is a painting by Georges Seurat. You can only see the dots if you look at it close up.

Here's a close-up of the grass. See the dots?

Paul Signac tried to get Vincent to paint with dots. Instead of just dots, Vincent tried something else. He painted with dashes and swirls.

While he was in Paris, Vincent saw some Japanese paintings. They really wowed him. Japanese artists painted with bright colors. They left the shadows out of their pictures. And they drew outlines around some things. Vincent's tried these ideas in his paintings.

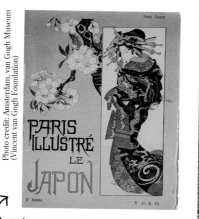

Vincent saw this magazine in Paris. To practice, he painted a copy of it.

Vincent's copy →

Japonaiserie, by Vincent van Gogh. Paris, 1887.
Photo credit: Amsterdam, van Gogh Museum (Vincent van Gogh Foundation)

Photo credit: Amsterdam, van Gogh Museum (Vincent van Gogh Foundation)

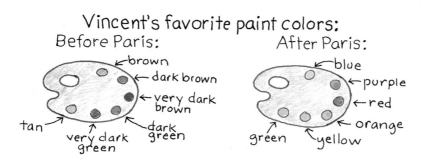

Vincent's favorite paint colors:

Before Paris:
←brown
←dark brown
←very dark brown
tan→
very dark green
dark green

After Paris:
←blue
←purple
←red
←orange
green
yellow

Best Buddies

The best thing about Paris was that Theo lived there, too. Vincent and his brother became roommates. Sounds great, huh? Wrong.

Vincent was a pest. He liked to argue. He was messy, too. Sometimes he just tried too hard. He got so excited about painting that he drove other people crazy.

Theo's friends didn't like Vincent. They wouldn't come over anymore. Theo wanted Vincent to move out. After two years, he finally did.

Vincent and Theo stayed best buddies, even though they fought a lot. Everyone else ignored Vincent's paintings. Theo always told him how good they were.

I agree with Theo. I think Vincent's pictures are great. Everything in them looks alive and moving—the sky, the trees, even people's clothes and skin!

Portrait of Père Tanguy, by Vincent van Gogh. 1887. Oil on canvas.
Photo credit: musée Rodin (photo by Jean de Calan)

This portrait is of Vincent's friend, Père Tanguy. He sold paint to artists in Paris. You can see Japanese art behind him.

Sunflowers

Vincent left Paris and headed south to Arles, France. He moved into a house that he shared for a while with another painter named Paul Gauguin. The house was yellow. Yellow was Vincent's favorite color.

Vincent painted all the time in Arles. He got better and better at it. He liked to paint pictures of people. But there was something else he liked to paint—flowers. Every morning, he got up early and picked a bunch of the yellow sunflowers that grew near his house.

The Yellow House, by Vincent van Gogh. Arles, 1888. Oil on canvas.
Photo credit: Amsterdam, van Gogh Museum (Vincent van Gogh Foundation)

Vincent painted this picture of his house in Arles.

Vincent would paint still-life pictures of the sunflowers until they got droopy. Sometimes he painted two sunflower pictures in one day!

His sunflower paintings look happy. I think he was in a good mood when he painted them.

Vase with sunflowers, by Vincent van Gogh. Arles, 1889.
Photo credit: Amsterdam, van Gogh Museum (Vincent van Gogh Foundation)

I feed sunflower seeds to birds in my yard.

This is called "Fourteen Sunflowers in a Vase."
(I count fifteen though.)

21

Work, Work, Work

The Postman Roulin, by Vincent van Gogh. Photo credit: Erich Lessing/Art Resource, NY.

Vincent was so busy working that he didn't make many friends. But he mailed so many letters that he did make friends with the postman, Joseph Roulin.

Vincent loved to work. One time, he painted 18 pictures in just 26 days. He painted fast because he wanted to get his feelings into the picture before he forgot them.

Vincent's paintings took weeks to dry because he put his paint on really thick. He even squirted it onto the picture straight from the tube when he was in a hurry.

He was always buying more paint. Paint, brushes, and canvas cost a lot of money. Sometimes Vincent had to choose between paint or food. He didn't have enough money for both. He chose paint. He must have really loved painting!

Theo wasn't rich either. But he believed in Vincent 100 percent. He wanted him to be able to paint as much as he wanted. So Theo bought as much paint as he could for Vincent. He even sent him an allowance. I don't know how much.

Weirdo?

Vincent didn't like to paint from his imagination. He usually went outside to paint things he saw. He painted all day in the hot sun. When it got dark, he stuck candles in his hat and just kept working.

The people in Arles thought Vincent was weird because he did things like that. As usual, Vincent didn't have many friends. He couldn't sell any paintings. He was lonely and sad.

I wonder if this mirror is the one
Vincent used to paint his self-portraits?

Vincent's shirts and hat
are hanging on the wall.

No closet,
I guess.

This is a picture Vincent painted of his room
in the yellow house in Arles.

My side
is clean
(usually).

My
brother's
mess.

I made this picture of my room. I have to
share with my brother like Vincent did with Theo.

25

One day, Vincent went a little crazy and cut off part of his ear. He gave it to a woman as a present. The police came and took him to a hospital. He almost died.

When he got better, he kept on painting. But he was never really the same after that.

Self-portrait with bandaged ear, by Vincent van Gogh. Photo credit: The Courtauld Institute Gallery, London.

Vincent wore a bandage on his ear
after he cut it.

If I met Vincent van Gogh, I would ask him three questions:

1. Were you sorry you cut off your ear?
2. Which one of your paintings do you like best?
3. What was the happiest day of your life?

And I would tell him something too: Don't worry if you don't sell any paintings right now. Someday you'll be famous.

Vincent the GREAT

I feel really sorry for Vincent van Gogh. He had an unhappy life. When he was 37 years old, he shot himself and died. That makes me sad.

I think it would make Vincent happy if he knew that people  love his paintings now. Theo's wife saved Vincent's paintings and letters. When her son grew up, he put them into a museum. Vincent became famous.

Photo credit: Amsterdam, van Gogh Museum (Vincent van Gogh Foundation)

Theo is buried next to Vincent.

Vincent van Gogh
was the biggest star of all!

The Starry Night, by Vincent van Gogh. 1889. Oil on canvas, 29 x 36¼".
The Museum of Modern Art, New York. Photograph © 2001 The Museum of Modern Art, New York.

Vincent named this picture "The Starry Night".
I like his swirly stars. I think it is his best painting.

Now Vincent's paintings are in museums all
over the world. I have never seen a real painting
by Vincent van Gogh. But I hope I will someday!

These are things that surprised

1. He wasn't rich.

2. He cut off part of his ear.
   I wish he hadn't done that.

3. He only sold one painting during his whole life. It was called *The Red Vineyards*.

The Red Vineyards at Arles, by Vincent van Gogh. 1888. Photo credit: Scala/Art Resource, NY.

me about Vincent van Gogh.

4. He was only an artist for ten years. He started when he was 27 and died when he was 37. He made over 1,700 drawings and paintings in that short time. That's almost one every two days!

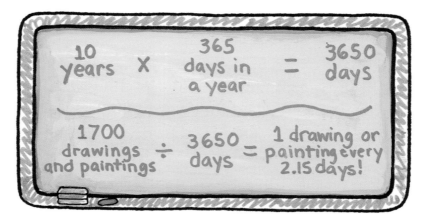

10 years X 365 days in a year = 3650 days

1700 drawings and paintings ÷ 3650 days = 1 drawing or painting every 2.15 days!

5. He thought the name "van Gogh" was hard to read. So he signed his pictures with just his first name. Like this:

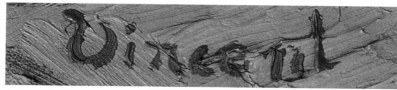

Detail from *Sunflowers*. Photo credits: Scala/Art Resource

These are words I learned
from reading about
Vincent van Gogh:

Portrait: a painting or picture of a person.

Self-portrait: a portrait a person makes of himself or herself.

Still-life: a painting or picture of things that are not alive (even if they used to be).

Brad, I am so impressed by how much you learned about Vincent van Gogh. Terrific work!
You might like to read <u>Vincent van Gogh</u> by Mike Venezia. It's a really good book.
Ms. Brandt